Animals in D

Illustrated by Pierre de Hugo
Created by Gallimard Jeunesse
and Pierre de Hugo

MOONLIGHT PUBLISHING / FIRST DISCOVERY

The dodo,
a funny-looking bird,
which used to live peacefully
on the Island of Mauritius
has completely disappeared.

It was easy prey for visiting sailors,
who shot and ate every single one of them.

Born on sandy beaches.
baby leatherback turtles have
to get into the safety of the
sea as fast as possible.

There are many sea-animals,
which are also now in danger
of disappearing altogether.

If they survive, the turtles
will come back many years
later as adults to lay their eggs
on the same beach.

Leatherback turtles can live for over 100 years.

In Europe the monk seal is being wiped out by pollution.

Ship's propellors are killing off the slow-moving manatees or sea-cows.

Although they are officially protected, whales are still being hunted for their meat and their blubber or fat.

The hump-backed whale helps its whale calf rise to the surface to breathe.

The white shark is the victim of its bad reputation with fishermen.

The blue whale is the biggest animal ever to have lived on earth.

A cœlacanth is a fish old enough to be found in marine fossils but it can still be found alive at sea today.

In Europe, farming and the spread of cities is destroying the natural habitat of many animals.

The giant hamster eats too much for the liking of farmers.

Pelicans are being poisoned by polluted water.

The brown bear which looks like your teddy bear...

The golden eagle like many
other birds of prey
is the victim of pesticides.

The wolf, which is not really
dangerous, has always
aroused fear in men.

... only survives in a few
mountain nature reserves.

The African elephant is dying out:
the ivory of its tusks is much sought after.

Here are some of the things we have been making out of ivory:
carved tusks, statues, billiard balls and domino pieces.

It is the rhinoceros's horn that
wildlife poachers are after.

In Africa
many other animals
are prey
to man's greed.

The mountain zebra can now
only be found in one nature reserve
in South Africa.

A mere
300 gorillas
survive today
in the forests of
Rwanda.

The aye-aye, which lives in Madagascar, gets its name from the sound it makes.

An okapi looks quite like a zebra but is more closely related to the giraffe.

The bald ibis is threatened by the overuse of pesticides.

In America species, which were widespread in the time of the Indians, have almost been wiped out.

Red wolves have been hunted down by farmers, because they attack their herds.

At the time of the opening up of the West, bison were hunted and slaughtered in great numbers.

The bald eagle with its white head is the symbol of the United States of America.

Most of the condors now living in California are in captivity.

Pumas, which lived all over America, can now only be found in parts of South and Central America.

On the American continent all these animals are in danger.

The black-footed ferret is hunted for its fur.

The American white crane is under threat: there are less than 200 left!

The sloth spends all day hanging from a branch asleep.

Chinchillas have become a protected species, because their fur was too much in demand.

The giant armadillo takes refuge in the shrinking Amazon forests.

Pandas, the best known of
the endangered species,
are very playful.

The giant panda is only
found in the mountains
of China and lives on
bamboo shoots.

Bamboos take 60 years to flower
and then they die.
A new shoot only appears 5 years later.

The shrinking of the
bamboo forests is a
serious threat to the
survival of pandas.

In Asia these animals are becoming fewer and fewer.

The Siberian tiger is the biggest of the cat family.

The Bactrian camel lives wild only in the Mongolian steppes.

The Japanese ibis is nearly extinct because of the damage done to its habitat and the destruction of its natural food supply.

Baby orang-utans are often separated from their mothers to be taken off to zoos.

A snow leopard's beautiful fur protects it from the cold but not from greedy poachers.

Koalas feed on
eucalyptus leaves.
They are becoming the victims
of deforestation.

A kakapo lays its eggs
on the ground where
they have no protection
from predators.

Australasia has many unusual animals.

The striped wallaby has almost disappeared in the wild.

A wombat is a marsupial, like a koala and a kangaroo.

The rabbit-eared bandicoot has been in decline since Australia was colonized.

FIRST DISCOVERY: OVER 125 TITLES AVAILABLE IN 5 SERIES

Translator: Penelope Stanley-Baker
ISBN 1 85103 334 3
© 2001 by Editions Gallimard Jeunesse
English text © 2002 by Moonlight Publishing Ltd
First published in the United Kingdom 2002
by Moonlight Publishing Limited, The King's Manor, East Hendred, Oxon. OX12 8JY
Printed in Italy by Editoriale Lloyd